AMAZING POWER

of

FORGIVENESS

BY
DOUG BATCHELOR

The Amazing Power of Forgiveness
By Doug Batchelor

Amazing Facts International
P.O. Box 1058, Roseville, CA 95678
afbookstore.com

Edited by Kristyn Dolinsky
Cover by Haley Trimmer
Layout by Jacob McBlane

ISBN: 978-1-952505-29-4

Table of Contents

Chapter 1

Introduction

An Amazing Fact: *As it became clear that the South would lose the Civil War, Abraham Lincoln turned his attention to the reunification of the country. The rift between the North and the South was deep, and the bloodiest war in American history had created profound division. To begin the healing process, Lincoln issued the Proclamation of Amnesty and Reconstruction, which called for a full pardon and restoration of property to all Southerners engaged in the rebellion. Lincoln knew the key to unity within the country would be in full and free forgiveness. A few months later, the president was assassinated by an embittered Southerner, John Wilkes Booth, who could not forgive.*

A World Without Forgiveness

What would the world be like without forgiveness?

It would be a very bleak and hopeless place indeed—never-ending hatred, resentment, feuds; punishment would be exacting, efficient.

Yet, in fact, our world is becoming more like that by the day, isn't it? We see lawsuits galore for even the most miniscule of faults—and some perhaps looking for fault where there is none. There is also "cancel culture," an intransigent practice of boycotting public and private figures for their offenses, whether true or not, whether the offense happened a decade ago or a day ago. The flaw is published, scrutinized, and then flogged down the aisles of social media. Who decides what an offense is and what is not? The one doing the cancelling decides.

Now, don't get me wrong. We all need accountability, law and order. But how would God judge someone suing a company over 11 percent of lip balm stuck at the bottom of the tube? True story. You start to see things—and people—differently when you're the one on trial, don't you?

What's Guilt Got to Do with It?

The good news for us is that before the great day of judgment comes, we have the opportunity—indeed, many opportunities—to receive God's forgiveness for our offenses. And His forgiveness

is crucial in the plan of salvation. Without it, you and I would be doomed.

What is forgiveness? It is one of God's responses to wrongdoing. When we do wrong, when we break God's law, it is called sin. In other words, "sin is lawlessness" (1 John 3:4).

What happens to our interaction with God when we sin? "Your iniquities have separated you from your God; and your sins have hidden His face from you, so that He will not hear" (Isaiah 59:2). That is how abhorrent sin is to God.

So, what do we do now? How do we get from this dark place to being forgiven? Well, it all begins with a little something called guilt. At some point in your life, if you have a conscience, you've felt guilt. It's that feeling of defilement, that awareness that you've done something wrong—and it's not a nice feeling, is it?

But guilt is actually the first step on the road to repentance. It's the alarm that indicates when you have strayed from the path of righteousness. Wouldn't you rather feel a little pain that tells you to stop touching the hot stove than no feeling at all that ends up burning you beyond repair?

All guilt is uncomfortable, but not all guilt is bad. It is, in fact, one of the mighty works of the Holy Spirit: "When He has come, He will convict the world of sin" (John 16:8). That conviction is

guilt. But forgiveness depends on how a person responds to that conviction.

Chapter 2

Being Forgiven

In order to better understand this process of forgiveness, let's look at the Parable of the Unforgiving Servant. Jesus shares this parable in response to a question posed by one of His disciples, Simon Peter, who asked, "Lord, how often shall my brother sin against me, and I forgive him? Up to seven times?" (Matthew 18:21).

In those days, the Jewish priests erroneously propagated the teaching that you were to forgive a person only up to three times. Some rabbis even taught that God forgave only three times, like baseball—three strikes, and you're out!

Peter, by picking the number seven, endeavored to impress Jesus with how gracious of a person he was. Why, seven times was more than double what was supposedly designated. Indeed, it was the number commonly symbolizing perfection or completeness. (For instance, the

biblical year of jubilee, a time when all debts were forgiven, occurred following a multiple of seven times seven years.) It seems that Peter hoped that Jesus would praise him in front of his peers for being so magnanimous. But Jesus' response was nothing of the kind.

He said, "I do not say to you, up to seven times, but up to seventy times seven" (v. 22).

Then Jesus went on to tell a powerful parable of a king's servant—let's call him Sidney—who had misappropriated 10,000 talents from the king-dom's treasury, we can imagine on anything from lavish expense accounts to gambling to full-on hedonism. When called on the carpet, Sidney was unable to pay the king back. Therefore, as was the custom, the king commanded that he and all he had be sold in an effort to recover at least some fraction of the debt. However, Sidney pleaded to the monarch, who ended up mercifully forgiving the man the entirety of his monumental debt.

Sadly, Sidney was indifferent to the compassion extended to him, so he went on to harass a fellow servant for a nominal debt—an amount minuscule compared to what he had owed the king. When the fellow servant could not pay, Sidney showed no mercy, throwing the man into debtor's prison.

However, the king's other servants, aware of this hypocritical cruelty, relayed the news to the

monarch, who in turn revoked Sidney's forgiveness of the first debt and threw him into debtor's prison as well, but not before reproaching him for his lack of compassion.

The king in this parable represents God, and Sidney represents men and women with a sinful human heart. The debt represents our sins and offenses against God. The lesson of the parable is a warning: "So My heavenly Father also will do to you if each of you, from his heart, does not forgive his brother his trespasses" (v. 35).

Who's on First?

Now, it is important that Christ's statement is not misunderstood. The parable defines two types of forgiveness: vertical and horizontal. Forgiveness between you and God, then forgiveness between you and another person. The sequence matters.

In the parable, it is the king who first forgives the servant. God is always the One who forgives us first. His forgiveness touches our hearts and initiates our forgiveness. "Beloved, if God so loved us, we also ought to love one another" (1 John 4:11).

In the Parable of the Prodigal Son, why do you think the father saw his son "when he was still a great way off"? (Luke 15:20). He had always been looking for his son; he was longing for him to return. When he finally spotted him, the father

didn't wait for his son to come to him but joyfully "ran" to meet him "and fell on his neck and kissed him." The father, a representation of God, was longing to forgive his son at the first sight of his return. His forgiveness had come first, even before the son could finish up his repentant apology.

Do not mistake Jesus' conclusion as some kind of *quid pro quo* between you and God. There is no deal in which you must offer forgiveness to each person who has wronged you in order for God to forgive you. Sidney did not have to jump through any hoops to receive the king's pardon; he was freely forgiven simply because the king wanted to forgive him. And that is the beauty of God's forgiveness. It is given when you are at your lowest, when you have nothing to offer, when you don't deserve it. The parable has the correct process: God forgives you first. Then it is up to you to embrace that forgiveness and pass it on.

The Better Savior

The glorious news is that we, without a doubt, have the assurance of God's forgiveness: "Oh, give thanks to the LORD, for He is good! For His mercy endures forever" (Psalm 106:1); "He will abundantly pardon" (Isaiah 55:7); "I said, 'I will confess my transgressions to the LORD,' and You forgave the iniquity of my sin" (Psalm 32:5); His mercy is

"as the heavens are high above the earth" (103:11). Are you convinced? Every time we repent, we can know that we have God's forgiveness. Every time we fail, God is willing and able to give forgiveness for it. His mercies and compassion are fresh every morning, and His faithfulness is great (Lamentations 3:22, 23). Friend, you are not a better sinner than Jesus is a Savior.

Moreover, God's forgiveness is always 100 percent. He "will cast all our sins into the depths of the sea" (Micah 7:19); He will remove them "as far as the east is from the west" (Psalm 103:12); "if we confess our sins, He is faithful and just to forgive us our sins and to cleanse us from all unrighteousness" (1 John 1:9).

There is no payment plan and no interest accrued. Paying back a loan is nothing but a business transaction; God is not your banker—He is your heavenly Father.

Let me illustrate this good news with a personal experience. Years ago, a new family began attending the small church I was pastoring. They sat in the front row every Sabbath, eager for the Word. And the father, who had a beautiful voice, would frequently sing for song service.

One day, the father, who had just opened an autobody shop, approached me for some financial advice, and, in the end, I ended up co-signing on a check he had received from an insurance company.

But a week later, the check was cancelled—and I was out $1,500. The father was mortified and promised that he would pay me back.

But his business was still struggling to make a profit. Weeks passed—with still no money in sight. And I began to notice little differences here and there. Every time I saw the family, the first thing the father would mention was the money he owed me. Even though I had not brought it up, he always did. There was this unspoken tension that kept building and building. As more time passed, I began to notice the family starting to sit farther back in church. One Sabbath, they did not come at all.

I realized what was happening. The member no longer saw me as his pastor; I was now his creditor. One day, as I was driving, a couple of Bible verses were impressed upon me: "Lend, hoping for nothing in return" (Luke 6:35), and, "Whatever you want men to do to you, do also to them" (Matthew 7:12). I confess it was hard to accept. I didn't want to write off $1,500. But at the end of the day, the Holy Spirit had convicted me: The souls of that man and his family were worth more than my money.

So, I forgave the father his debt. It took some convincing—for myself as well as him. But God enabled me to let it go. It was as though a huge weight had melted from their shoulders, and in

a sense, it had. The father and I were able to start over. The next Sabbath, the family was back in the frontmost pew, and the father was singing his heart out.

Do you see what forgiveness singlehandedly did? The loan had effectually canceled out any Christian influence I had with them. I had ceased to become their pastor; I was simply someone who—though not purposefully—caused them to feel shame. Forgiveness restored our spiritual relationship. We, likewise, can love God once we stop seeing Him as Someone who cares about what we owe and start seeing Him as Someone who cares about who we are.

What You Really Want

God's forgiveness is wider than the ocean, deeper than an abyss, higher than the tallest mountain. But our hearts are not. The problem lies with our capacity to repent. While God always forgives, the tragedy is that we may not always want His forgiveness.

Hebrews 3:13 warns us of this danger: "Exhort one another daily, while it is called 'Today,' lest any of you be hardened through the deceitfulness of sin." And Hebrews 10:26 declares, "If we sin willfully after we have received the knowledge of the truth, there no longer remains a sacrifice for

sins." (In the Greek, this verse has the connotation of continuous sinning, the deliberate prolonging of sin.)

Don't ever presume to know how your heart will be a day or a week or a year down the road. Don't be so sure that you will be able to turn on a dime whenever you like. Paul reasoned, "What shall we say then? Shall we continue in sin that grace may abound? Certainly not! How shall we who died to sin live any longer in it?" (Romans 6:1, 2). This was obvious to the apostle, but it will not be so to the person who has ceased to realize that what he is doing is sin.

Sin is something like leprosy, a disease that gradually deadens a person's nervous system. This system is our body's central mode of communication; our nerves send information to other parts of our body, especially to our brain, letting us know when we put our hands on a hot surface or stub our toe in the middle of the night.

With leprosy, however, the nerve sensations in a person's extremities begin to fail. If a friend accidentally steps on his toes, a leper doesn't realize it. If a 50-ton block of cement fell on his toes, the leper still wouldn't know the difference. Eventually, if left unattended, leprosy could even cause a person to go blind (because they forget to blink) or lose his extremities through injury—all

because his warning system was not functioning properly.

Like sin, leprosy often starts off small and largely unnoticeable. Gradually though, it spreads (Leviticus 13:8) and eats up the person from the inside out. Sin, likewise, starts in "the heart" (Matthew 15:19); "then, when desire has conceived, it gives birth to sin; and sin, when it is full-grown, brings forth death" (James 1:15). The Bible details that one of the results of having leprosy was separation from society: "He is unclean, and he shall dwell alone; his dwelling shall be outside the camp" (Leviticus 13:46). Sin similarly separates us from God (Isaiah 59:2)—and each other.

If leprosy symbolizes sin, then the sensations of pain from our nerves would be conviction of the Holy Spirit—a guilty conscience. Just like nerves begin to deaden as leprosy spreads, the less conviction a person feels the more he indulges in sin, the more it spreads and takes hold of him. He gets used to the sin and drowns out the guilt, little by little, until he doesn't feel it anymore, even when that sin has him by the throat.

This is what leads to the unpardonable sin, a person's willful and repeated ignoring of the Holy Spirit, as in Hebrews 10:26. Jesus said, "He who blasphemes against the Holy Spirit never has forgiveness" (Mark 3:29)—not because

God will not offer it, but because the person himself will not desire it nor ask for it.

The Enormity of Sin

Between 1997 and 2003, the U.S. Department of Defense spent more than $100 million on 270,000 commercial airline tickets that were never used. But this egregious example of government waste—which left taxpayers less than thrilled—was nothing when compared to the 10,000 talents Sidney owed the king in the parable.

In America today, 10,000 talents of gold would be upwards of $4.5 billion. Now, maybe in comparison to our national debt, that seems like peanuts. But let me put this in perspective: In the days when Jesus walked the earth, the total amount of taxes the entire Jewish nation paid annually to the Roman Empire was roughly 2,000 talents, a fifth of the total that Sidney owed the king. My point is that 10,000 talents represented an obscene amount of money. On top of that, it was squandered not by a department or a country but by a single employee.

But perhaps you're still thinking it wouldn't be such a big deal. In America, at least, a person—or even a business—can file for bankruptcy, and you're basically good to go. Sure, your credit is shot, and there may be repayment plans, but it's

not the soul-wrenching, lifelong devastation that such a problem was in Bible times.

The Scriptures tell the story about a widow in debt who told Elisha the prophet, "The creditor is coming to take my two sons to be his slaves" (2 Kings 4:1). This was a normal consequence. Not only could a creditor take all you owned, he could also take you and your family as his slaves. Sidney, his entire family, and all his assets would have been sold into slavery had not the king had mercy on him.

But it was not only enslavement. Debtors could also be thrown into jail. Once inside, they were then tortured by the prison keepers in accordance with how much they owed. For Sidney, owing 10,000 talents, well, even a lifetime of torture would not cover his debt to the king.

Don't miss this point. This was a colossal debt that Sidney could never pay back. His life was at stake. No matter how long he lived or how hard he worked, he could never repay that deficit—and that's just like our debt of sin. Sidney's was a debt that only the one to whom he was indebted could choose to forgive. Yes, just like sin. There is a reason why the vertical piece on the cross is always longer than the horizontal: God forgives so much more than we will ever have to—in every sense of the word.

No one has forgiven more than Jesus, but do you realize that means that no one has been hurt more than Jesus either? When you sin, though there may be others you hurt, the One who is unfailingly and incontrovertibly wronged is God. His is the relationship you always damage; He is the One who is ultimately pained. Even though David had an adulterous affair with Bathsheba and though he had murdered Uriah, David simply stated, "I have sinned against the LORD" (2 Samuel 12:13).

The king in the parable was the one who absorbed that irretrievable loss. The prodigal son wasted nearly half of his father's life savings (Luke 15:12, 14); when he returned, his father was the one who bore the loss. But think about this: The father did not consider it a loss. Instead, he calculated that having his son home safe and sound was of infinitely more value to him.

Chapter 3

The Deathtrap of the Legalistic Mind

Do you find it strange that the unforgiving servant, Sidney, didn't seem to comprehend that the king had truly forgiven him? What happened? Let's start with his reaction to his own guilt.

Right off the bat, Sidney seems insincere. He did not take the initiative to confess his crime but instead "was brought to" the king (Matthew 18:24), meaning he waited to rectify his mess until he was caught. Once he was exposed, he even had the audacity to say to the king, "Master, have patience with me, and I will pay you all" (v. 26).

Did you notice that he didn't ask for forgiveness for his poor management of the king's resources? All he asked for was time—time to work off a debt he could never possibly repay. It was the king, out

of his own compassion, who mercifully extended full forgiveness.

This story also reveals the mindset of a proud legalist. Sidney was given a gift, but he saw it only as a loan and determined to pay it back. Yet can anyone truly work off their sins? Do you think you can earn your way to heaven? The Bible is clear: It is impossible. Eternal life is a gift given to a sinner only by the forgiveness of God through the blood of Jesus Christ: "In Him we have redemption through His blood, the forgiveness of sins" (Ephesians 1:7). Tragically, a person with this mindset has been offered forgiveness but doesn't believe it or trust in God's provision.

A legalist is much like an amputee with phantom pain, a condition in which the sufferer feels pain from a limb that is gone—the pain is entirely "in his head," as it were. A legalist feels he must repay a sin debt that has already been paid and, therefore, he remains in bondage to a phantom debt. With such a mindset, a person exalts his own judgment above God's, which is a form of blasphemy (John 10:33).

Famed Reformer Martin Luther was said to have had a dream illustrating forgiveness. While various versions of this story are floating around, this is the gist: In the dream, Luther found himself being accused by Satan, who unrolled a long scroll containing a list of Luther's sins and held it before

the young believer. On reaching the end of the scroll, Luther asked the devil, "Is that all?"

"No," the devil replied.

Satan then revealed a second scroll and, after that, a third. But now the devil had no more scrolls.

"You've forgotten something," Luther exclaimed.

He then triumphantly wrote on each scroll, "The blood of Jesus Christ cleanses us from all sins." Luther was known for his adherence to the doctrine of justification by faith: "For by grace you have been saved through faith, and that not of yourselves; it is the gift of God, not of works" (Ephesians 2:8, 9). In other words, when God says you are forgiven, you can trust Him!

Pride and Precipice

A person with a legalistic mindset has too much confidence in his own abilities, too much belief in his own sin-sick heart. In a way, he doesn't believe God can provide for him as well as he can provide for himself. This is pride.

Sidney must have held a position of some importance. To have had even an opportunity to squander 10,000 talents, he must have been a high-ranking official with his own servants. Imagine, then, how humiliating it must have

been for him to grovel at the king's feet, like a dog begging for mercy (Matthew 18:26). The courtiers and his peers were watching, maybe even some of his assistants. It would have been mortifying for a proud man!

What would it be like to see your boss or mentor or even your pastor groveling for clemency for some company or church embezzlement scheme? You'd probably lose all respect for the person. Needless to say, at this point, Sidney's reputation was pretty much ruined. Have you noticed that when someone is full of pride, he cannot bear to be embarrassed? He thinks a lot of himself. He absolutely cannot stand to be wrong, especially in front of other people, and often, he gets defensive.

Such was the case with Sidney, our unforgiving servant. He "went out and found one of his fellow servants who owed him a hundred denarii" (v. 28) and viciously demanded payment. Did you catch that? He didn't just happen to run into the other servant; Sidney hunted him down! Then, "he laid hands on him and took him by the throat, saying, 'Pay me what you owe!'"

That's a staggering reaction considering the amount his servant owed him. Today, 100 denarii is the equivalent to about $44. In Jesus' day, that would have been about a week's wages. But Sidney could not forgive it; he could not let it go. The king

had just forgiven him 10,000 talents, but he could not forgive a debt of pocket change!

Think about this. The distance between the earth and the sun is about 92 million miles. This represents God's forgiveness toward us. God is willing to forgive us 92 million miles, yet we often struggle to forgive each other of a single inch!

If I had been forgiven 10,000 talents, I would be busy kissing the king's feet or celebrating at home with the family I had almost lost—not out strangling my co-worker for a mere 100 denarii.

But, in reality, this had nothing to do with the other servant or his 100 denarii, and everything to do with Sidney's concept of the king. He doubted that the king had freely forgiven him and assumed he still had to work off his debt. Although he had already been forgiven, he believed he still had to earn that forgiveness.

It is only in believing in the grace and full mercy of God that a believer's heart can be transformed. Sidney did not believe, so his heart was not changed.

On the Defense

The prideful heart cannot endure guilt. Its self-deceptive reputation is at stake. It will, like a wild animal, claw in rabid panic, blind to friend or foe. Ultimately, it must destroy anything in its

path. In the end, the sinful heart self-destructs. With Sidney's unforgiving heart running wild, we last see him losing his family and his property, ultimately ending up in jail being tortured (v. 30). Other accounts in the Bible reveal the heinous result of guilt upon a prideful heart.

In the case of Cain and Abel, Adam and Eve's first two children, both sons brought an offering to God. But Abel's offering, a sacrifice from his flock, was in obedience to God's will, whereas Cain's, a harvest from his fields, was not (Genesis 4:3–5).

Perhaps you might be thinking that Cain's offering seems nicer. He didn't have to kill anything; there was no blood, no mess, no gore. Instead, he just picked some lovely fruit and vegetables from his garden. Doesn't that "seem" like a more considerate gift for God?

But that was exactly the point.

Scripture unequivocally states that "without shedding of blood there is no remission" of sin (Hebrews 9:22). Remission means forgiveness. It is a fact that "the wages of sin is death" (Romans 6:23). To be forgiven our sins, blood must be shed—but if not ours, then whose? Abel's gift demonstrated that he understood that there was to be a Substitute that would die in our place so that we could receive forgiveness. The sacrifice he brought was a symbol of that Substitute, his

humble acknowledgement that he was a sinner in need of a Savior.

But it was not so with Cain. Cain brought the work of his own hands, what he had tilled, what he had sown and grown. His offering was actually an arrogant dismissal of the Savior, an insolence that boasted of his own effort to remove the blight of sin. And it was not accepted by God.

When confronted with the truth, Cain could have repented, as King David did when confronted with his sin. He could have confessed his pride and selfishness. But he didn't. Instead, he got angry. He went to his brother Abel, a pillar of obedience next to his own disobedience. When his younger brother tried to reason with him, Cain's offended pride exploded, and he killed his brother (Genesis 4:8).

Cain didn't care about what he had done to dishonor God. He cared that someone else had made his wrongdoing apparent. More often than not, a person knows when he has done something wrong. But it is when he conceals his own guilty conscience from himself that the real trouble begins. Cain wanted to destroy that feeling of guilt, so he took it out on the one person who made him look morally deficient.

"If anyone thinks himself to be something, when he is nothing, he deceives himself" (Galatians 6:3). Pride will always eagerly point

the finger at someone else. Might Sidney have deceived himself into believing his fellow servant was to blame for all his troubles?

Let's look at another example. Hoping to ensnare Jesus in a doctrinal trap, Jewish leaders indicted a woman caught in adultery. Instead of entering into their debate, Jesus held up a mirror to show them their own sins, writing them in the sand at their feet (John 8:6, 8). He replied, "He who is without sin among you, let him throw a stone at her first" (v. 7).

Thus, the scribes and the Pharisees, like Cain, were faced with their own guilt. Here they were passing judgment on a woman for her sin—a sin in which, as part of their devilish plan, they had been accomplices. Scripture says that as Jesus wrote in the sand, they were "convicted by their conscience" (v. 9); in other words, they felt guilty.

Ultimately, the woman's life was spared—but instead of changing their hearts, this instance only served to deepen the Jewish leaders' rage against Christ. This could have been a golden opportunity for each of them to come to Jesus, asking forgiveness of their sins laid bare. But all they did with their guilt was project it onto someone else. They could not accept their own faults; after all, as "men of God," they considered themselves beacons before the sinful masses. They resented Jesus' goodness; it magnified their badness. Their guilt

only hardened their resolve to kill the Messiah, the sacrificial Lamb.

Even after Christ's death, their path of carnage continued in persecuting the apostles and the stoning of Stephen, a disciple who rebuked them for their culpability in the crucifixion. As he himself stood trial for blasphemy, Stephen said to them:

> You stiff-necked and uncircumcised in heart and ears! You always resist the Holy Spirit; as your fathers did, so do you. Which of the prophets did your fathers not persecute? And they killed those who foretold the coming of the Just One [Jesus Christ], of whom you now have become the betrayers and murderers (Acts 7:51–53).

This statement laid out their guilt before the Jewish Supreme Court, and "when they heard these things they were cut to the heart" (v. 54). It was the Holy Spirit who was convicting them of sin—the Word of God, that double-edged sword, was piercing their very souls (Hebrews 4:12).

They had reached yet another spiritual crossroad. Would they admit their fault? Alas, no; instead, "they cried out with a loud voice, stopped their ears, and ran at [Stephen] with one accord; and they cast him out of the city and stoned him"

(Acts 7:57, 58). They had to silence the source of their guilt.

It is said that written on the inside of renowned Christian author John Bunyan's Bible were these words: "This book will keep you from sin, or sin will keep you from this book." Did you know that there are those who use this reasoning to not attend church? They don't go anywhere that makes them feel a little guilty or uncomfortable or bad about themselves. But the problem with that solution is that it does not make the sin go away. Instead, the sin grows bigger; it infiltrates deeper. When we allow such pride to stifle our guilt, aren't we blocking our chance at eternal life?

Guilt Done Wrong

I'd like to pause here to issue a warning. Stephen was the one pointing out the guilty, but—and don't miss this—he was "full of the Holy Spirit" (v. 55). The Holy Spirit is the One who knows how and when to convict people of sin. We do not. It is our duty as Christians to check our motives against the promptings of the Holy Spirit, to approach rebuke prayerfully and with humility.

Are you reproaching your brother while there is "a plank … in your own eye"? (Matthew 7:4). Are you ignoring your own guilt or even transferring it onto someone else? Are you doing it with

pride—or even a little bit of glee? If you are, then you have no business doing it. "Hypocrite!" Jesus declared, "First remove the plank from your own eye, and then you will see clearly to remove the speck from your brother's eye" (v. 5). If you are going to rebuke someone, be led by the Spirit; do it in love, with that person's eternal fate in mind.

People often use guilt to get what they want. How many times have salespeople used that technique to get a customer to buy a product? Even pastors sometimes do it. It's manipulative, but it often works. It shows how powerful the feeling of guilt is, and it shows that guilt can be abused. That is not the kind of guilt brought by the Holy Spirit; neither is that the guilt that leads to repentance.

Chapter 4

Guilt Done Right

When you don't give your sin to God, it's your sin. You are the one dealing with it; you are the one managing it. That puts a lot of stress on you. A guilty conscience wears on a person. Some react in outbursts of anger; some withdraw from life in shame; others live in strict denial; yet others harbor fear, always looking over their shoulder, living in constant worry of divine retribution. But all have something in common: They did not take their sins to God.

In the parable of the Pharisee and the tax collector, the Pharisee arrogantly prayed, "God, I thank You that I am not like other men …, [such] as this tax collector" (Luke 18:11). He did not actually thank God; he merely praised himself. His concern was focused on how he looked, how he compared; his prayer was filled with what he had done (v. 12). His was the ultimate self-centered, legalistic mind.

By contrast, the tax collector who the Pharisee had just disparaged was focused solely on God—God's goodness, God's grace, God's magnificence. He "would not so much as raise his eyes to heaven, but beat his breast, saying, 'God, be merciful to me a sinner!'" (v. 13).

This is the manner in which God desires for us to respond to guilt. He desires us not to take up arms but to surrender. Peter exclaimed, "Depart from me, for I am a sinful man, O Lord" (5:8). He saw what Christ was capable of in relation to his own efforts, and it brought him to his knees. Give your sin to Jesus. Give it to Him to handle. He is the only One who can blot that sin out. But it is your choice. You must bring it to Him.

"If we confess our sins, He is faithful and just to forgive us our sins and to cleanse us from all unrighteousness" (1 John 1:9). Note that this confession is not merely a declaration of wrongdoing. A criminal can admit to a murder nonchalantly or boastfully—or even as a strategy for securing a plea bargain. But true confession goes hand in hand with repentance and a sorrow for sin. When someone repents, he "[turns] from all [his] transgressions" (Ezekiel 18:30); "he who covers his sin will not prosper, but whoever confesses and forsakes them will have mercy" (Proverbs 28:13). This is the confession that begets forgiveness.

The prophet Isaiah confessed, "Woe is me, for I am undone! Because I am a man of unclean lips" (Isaiah 6:5). It was because Isaiah had brought his sin to God that He could then immediately cleanse him of it: "Your iniquity is taken away, and your sin purged" (v. 7).

Guilt to Gratitude

Returning briefly to the story of the woman caught in adultery, who was the other guilty party in the account? The woman herself! She had been caught red-handed.

Many believe this woman to have been Mary Magdalene and this account to be her first encounter with Jesus. What did Mary do with her guilt? Ironically, she did the opposite of her accusers.

After the embarrassed Pharisees and scribes left, Jesus remained with Mary, who stood helplessly before Him. He assured her that He did not condemn her, but He also instructed her, "Go and sin no more" (John 8:11).

This is the gospel in a nutshell. Mary was guilty. According to the law, she should have died for her offense. But Christ gave her a reprieve. When we see Mary again, she's washing Jesus' feet with her tears, wiping them with her hair (Luke 7:38); she is sitting at Jesus' feet, listening to him teach (10:39); she is the first disciple at His tomb the Sunday

after His death (John 20:1). Christ's forgiveness caused her to come to Him, not run from Him. It turned her guilt into gratitude, her gratitude into devotion.

You Are the Man

King David was not innocent either. He had an affair with a married woman, the wife of a friend no less, and when she became pregnant, in an attempt to cover up his deed, he devised that her husband be sent on a suicide mission. What's more, he ordered the commander of his army to do the dirty work for him.

But "the eyes of the LORD are in every place" (Proverbs 15:3). David's own crime was relayed to him by the prophet Nathan in the form of a story. In the parable told him, a rich man who owned multitudes of cattle seized—not his own—but a poor man's only beloved lamb to have for dinner.

Indignant, David condemned the rich man for his vast injustice: "As the LORD lives, the man who has done this shall surely die!" (2 Samuel 12:5).

To this, Nathan replied, "You are the man!" (v. 7).

David was thunderstruck. His blatant guilt stared him in the face. He could have denied it. He could have blamed Bathsheba for bathing on the roof, or he could have let Joab take the fall for

Uriah's murder. He could have executed Nathan for daring to confront him. But David did none of that. Instead, he admitted his guilt: "I have sinned against the LORD" (v. 13).

For David's repentance, Nathan assured the king of God's forgiveness: "The LORD also has put away your sin; you shall not die."

Memorialized in one of the most famous psalms is David's confession: "For I acknowledge my transgressions, and my sin is always before me" (Psalm 51:3). With his acknowledgement came the realization that he could never stop sinning on his own. This thought drove him to the One who could help him to stop—Jesus Christ: "Deliver me from the guilt of bloodshed, O God, the God of my salvation" (v. 14).

Saving Shame

In the early days of the Christian church, the apostle Peter, upon healing a lame man at the temple in Jerusalem, took the opportunity to preach to those who had gathered to behold the miracle. Interestingly enough, his sermon was not unlike the one Stephen gave that led to his martyrdom.

The God of our fathers ... glorified His Servant Jesus, whom you delivered up and denied in the presence of Pilate, when he was determined to let Him go. But you denied the Holy One and the Just, and asked for a murderer to be granted to you, and killed the Prince of life (Acts 3:13–15).

The apostle certainly didn't mince words, openly placing the blame of Christ's death upon their nation. But he didn't stop there. He instructed them as to how to handle their guilt: "Repent therefore and be converted, that your sins may be blotted out, so that times of refreshing may come from the presence of the Lord, and that He may send Jesus Christ" (vv. 19, 20).

The people could have rushed at him like the Jewish leaders did to Stephen. They easily outnumbered him and his companion, the apostle John; they could have slain them in minutes. But they didn't. Peter's words, directed by the Holy Spirit, convicted them, and they repented; "many of those who heard the word believed" (4:4). Their acceptance of their own guilt led to their repentance, which led to their conversion.

Guilt Versus Shame

Now, a distinction must be made. Feeling guilty is not the same thing as being ashamed.

When God has forgiven you, you no longer need to feel guilty, but you can still be ashamed of what you have done. Who likes dwelling on embarrassing situations or thinking about the times you have mistreated people? But you don't have to punish yourself for those deeds. Conversely, being forgiven does not give you license to do that sin again. If you believe you're forgiven, it does not suddenly make doing that sin okay. If you stop feeling guilty, it does not mean that the sin isn't still awful.

The devil is the one who wants us to continue in these never-ending cycles. He wants us to continue condemning ourselves or continue in the old sins. He wants us to continue believing that God cannot or will not forgive our sins and that all we have to count on is ourselves.

But do you know what Jesus wants? Jesus wants each of us to be reborn in Him. He promises to give us this new birth: "Therefore, if anyone is in Christ, he is a new creation; old things have passed away; behold, all things have become new" (2 Corinthians 5:17).

If Christ has made you a new person, do you still feel guilty for all the sins the old person did? Isn't that old person an entirely different person than who you are now? It would be similar to reading about a horrible crime in the newspaper.

You feel sorrow for the wickedness done, but you don't feel guilt. Someone else did the crime.

Again, this is not to say that you forget the evil of the sins you yourself have done. Indeed, it is just this understanding that helps to spur one's hatred of sin.

The Process of Forgiveness

So—is that it? I'm forgiven, and then I go my merry way? When Jesus instructed Mary, "Go and sin no more" (John 8:11), did she stop sinning, just like that? No, Jesus had to "cast seven demons" out of her (Mark 16:9). There are some people out there who will tell you otherwise, but the process of forgiveness is what the Christian walk is all about.

The fact is, the closer you draw to the holy presence of Christ, the more guilt you recognize—and consequently, the more grace as well. Scripture likens "the path of the just … [to] the shining sun, that shines ever brighter unto the perfect day" (Proverbs 4:18). Smudges and spots easily covered in the dimness of twilight become glaringly obvious at noonday. In like manner, the closer you get to "the Sun of Righteousness" (Malachi 4:2), the more light falls upon your unrighteousness.

The process of sanctification is this realization over and over again. But, mind you, a process means that you are on a road to somewhere, not on a treadmill going nowhere. The goal is not to stay guilty: "A righteous man may fall seven times and rise again" (Proverbs 24:16). If seven represents completeness, then that means every time you fall, Christ refines you a little bit more: "He who has begun a good work in you will *complete* it until the day of Jesus Christ" (Philippians 1:6, emphasis mine).

Peter had been walking with Jesus for three and a half years when he denied Him (Luke 22:55–62). After Peter repented and Jesus forgave him for those denials (John 21:15–17), Peter went on to fearlessly proclaim Christ in the early Christian church. This was not someone caught in the same cycle of sin, feeling the same guilt over and over. This was someone who was walking "the path of the just."

Guilt-Free

The ultimate goal for the believer is to not feel guilt at all. The ideal is to never be ashamed because you aren't doing anything of which to be ashamed. A famous Danish proverb says, "No one can be caught in places he does not visit." Don't even go there!

Philip Brooks, known for writing the lyrics to "O Little Town of Bethlehem," once wrote of how crucial it was "to keep clear of concealment, to keep clear of the need of concealment. ... It is an awful hour when the first necessity of hiding anything comes. The whole life is different thenceforth. When there are questions to be feared and eyes to be avoided and subjects that must not be touched, then the bloom of life is gone."

Job said, "My righteousness I hold fast, and will not let it go; my heart shall not reproach me as long as I live" (Job 27:6). Why did God count Job as "a blameless and upright man, one who fears God and shuns evil" (1:8)? It was not because Job was sinless. It was what Job did with his sins that allowed his heart to not reproach him. Job offered sacrifices to God; he confessed and asked forgiveness for his sins—and he interceded for his family's sins as well. This "Job did regularly" (v. 5). Job's life—his weaknesses, his faults—was an open book to God.

So, while guilt from sin can be used for our own good, it is better not to feel guilt at all. The apostle John assures us, "Beloved, if our heart does not condemn us, we have confidence toward God" (1 John 3:21). Of course, ultimately in heaven, all of the former painful memories and guilt will no longer be thought about. "For behold, I create new

heavens and a new earth; and the former shall not be remembered or come to mind" (Isaiah 65:17).

Chapter 5

Forgiveness in Prophecy

Let's return to Peter's original question, the one that triggered the parable of the unforgiving servant in the first place. "Lord, how often shall my brother sin against me, and I forgive him? Up to seven times?" (Matthew 18:21). So, Peter's question was actually regarding a quantity of our forgiveness of one another—horizontal forgiveness.

Jesus' response was telling: "I do not say to you, up to seven times, but up to seventy times seven" (v. 22).

Let's do the math: 70 multiplied by 7 equals 490. So, does that mean we should forgive one another 490 times? Is that what Jesus was saying? That doesn't make sense. That would be just like the Pharisees' method of counting sins, only it would require an even more laborious tracking system. Let's examine what Christ really meant.

The 490-Year Prophecy

The other book in the Bible where this specific number, 490, appears is in Daniel. The angel Gabriel foretold, "Seventy weeks are determined for your people and for your holy city" (Daniel 9:24).

There is a set rule for prophetic time in the Bible: Each prophetic day equals one literal year. (See Numbers 14:34; Ezekiel 4:6.) Thus, the 70 weeks are not 70 literal weeks; they are 70 *prophetic* weeks. Seventy prophetic weeks equal 490 literal years. This is done by multiplying the number of weeks, 70, by the number of days in a week, seven—the exact equation with which Jesus responded to Peter. Hence, this prophecy found in Daniel is known as the 490-year prophecy.

From what Gabriel said, we can conclude that "seventy weeks," or 490 years, were set aside for a specific purpose and for a specific people, Daniel's people. As Daniel was Hebrew (Daniel 1:3, 6), his "people" meant the Jewish nation. Interesting. So, the Jewish nation had 490 years to do what?

The verse continues: "to finish the transgression, to make an end of sins, to make reconciliation for iniquity, to bring in everlasting righteousness, to seal up vision and prophecy, and to anoint the Most Holy" (9:24). That sounds like an important purpose, doesn't it? But what did it all mean?

The Jewish nation was God's chosen people. To them was given the express privilege of witnessing to the world about the Almighty God. But the Jews had largely failed in this matter. Instead, they rebelled against the Lord multiple times, joining themselves to heathen nations and worshiping their idols. By the time Gabriel gave Daniel this prophecy, Israel had been in Babylonian captivity for nearly 70 years.

But Daniel had a burden for his people. Through prayer, he made intercession for himself and his nation: "To the Lord our God belong mercy and forgiveness, though we have rebelled against Him. … We have sinned, we have done wickedly! … O Lord, forgive!" (v. 9, 15, 19).

And because of Daniel's sincere prayer and repentance, God answered by disclosing the 70-week prophecy. Gabriel relayed, "At the beginning of your supplications the command went out, and I have come to tell you" (v. 23).

Thus, the 490 years given to the Jewish nation were an act of mercy of God. Israel had not yet passed the point of no return; they still had a chance to turn from and "make an end of sins," to ask for forgiveness.

But that was not all.

The Crux of Forgiveness

In the last prophetic week of those 490 years, God did something unique. He separated out the first 483 years from the last seven—in other words, the first 69 prophetic weeks from the last prophetic week. In this last prophetic week, the Messiah, Jesus Christ, would begin and complete His public ministry, culminating in His death on the cross: "Until Messiah the Prince, there shall be seven weeks and sixty-two weeks" (v. 25). This was the crux of the prophecy. Jesus' sacrifice was what made forgiveness possible: "This is My blood of the new covenant," Christ said, "which is shed for many for the remission of sins" (Matthew 26:28). His blood was what "[made] reconciliation for iniquity"; His blood was what "[brought] in everlasting righteousness." He was made "to be sin for us" so that we would have the opportunity of "eternal life in Christ Jesus our Lord" (2 Corinthians 5:21; Romans 6:23).

By referencing the 490-year prophecy in His answer to Peter, Jesus was actually pointing to Himself as the One who provides forgiveness for all. When you realize the monumental act to which Christ condescended for you, when you think about what it took—what He left, what He lost—what happens to your heart? "The goodness of God leads [us] to repentance" (2:4). His grace

48

is not cheap. Do you value it? Do you understand its worth? Do you realize how much God loves you? It is because He loves you that He paid off your debt of sin.

San Francisco is famous for its streetcars. In fact, the city runs the only manually operated cable car system in the entire world. But unfortunately, the cars are also prone to a high rate of accidents, averaging about one a month.

In one such incident several years ago, a pedestrian had not only been knocked down by a streetcar, but the poor man had also become trapped underneath its axle. The pedestrian was still alive, but he was horribly wounded.

A large crowd gathered around the bleeding and scared man. "Help is on the way," some told him. Others peered under the car just to gawk at him. But then a businessman, dressed in a sharp, pristine suit, came forward. He dropped to his hands and knees and crawled on the dirty street under the greasy chassis of the bus, lying down next to the injured man. The businessman put his hand on the man's shoulder and said, "I'm going to stay here with you until help arrives. You're going to make it."

That is the difference between pity and compassion. Pity looks down; compassion gets down. That is what Jesus showed us— compassion. In the parable, it was the king who

"was moved with compassion" (Matthew 18:27). The father "had compassion" for his prodigal son (Luke 15:20). In all of Scripture, this Greek word for "compassion" is used only in reference to Jesus: "God demonstrates His own love toward us, in that while we were still sinners, Christ died for us" (Romans 5:8).

Forgiveness is the miracle that results from such love. Not only does God's forgiveness bestow the gift of eternal life, but it is the catalyst that transforms our hearts: "We love Him because He first loved us" (1 John 4:19). About Mary Magdalene, Jesus said, "Her sins, which are many, are forgiven, for she loved much. But to whom little is forgiven, the same loves little" (Luke 7:47). Christ's compassion for Mary caused her to love Him much and bring her sins to Him in repentance.

It is also Christ's forgiveness for us that fuels our forgiveness for others: "God was in Christ reconciling the world to Himself, not imputing their trespasses to them, and has committed to us the word of reconciliation" (2 Corinthians 5:19). Suddenly, all the comparatively petty offenses of others shrink into insignificance. Christ gives us the capability to pass forgiveness onto others that they may see Christ's love too. "Even as Christ forgave you, so you also must do" (Colossians 3:13); "[forgive] one another, even as God in Christ

forgave you" (Ephesians 4:32). His forgiveness is our example and impetus.

The Full Cup

Sadly though, Daniel's people, the Jewish nation, did not "finish the transgression"; they continued in it. They were the ones to crucify the Messiah. Then, three-and-a-half years after Christ's death, the supreme court of the nation murdered Stephen. They had filled up their cup of iniquity. Thus, in AD 34, in the 490th year of the prophecy, the Jewish nation was "cut off" as God's special people—and the apostles took the gospel to the Gentiles. The 490-year prophecy reached its fulfillment.

But it does not have to be so for billions of souls in the world today. If you have not yet felt the pangs of your own guilt and laid your sins at the foot of the cross, this is Christ's plea to you, "for the LORD your God is gracious and merciful, and will not turn His face from you if you return to Him" (2 Chronicles 30:9). Will you allow God to forgive you and to create in you a clean heart, one that loves Him and others?

Chapter 6

Vengeance Is Not Mine

We know that the main character of the parable Jesus told Peter is Sidney, the unforgiving servant, but let's not forget his fellow perpetrator. The debt the other servant owed was, albeit, small in comparison; however, let me ask you a question: What if the other servant owed Sidney 10,000 denarii instead of 100? Would Sidney's reaction have then been justified?

Let's put that question in spiritual terms. What if someone did something really bad to you? What if someone really hurt you? Would you seek to get even? Would you make him pay for the rest of his life? Even if he begged for forgiveness and promised to make things right, would you do as Sidney did "and [throw] him into prison till he should pay the debt"? (Matthew 18:30).

"The LORD is a God of justice" (Isaiah 30:18) —right? "He administers justice for the fatherless and the widow" (Deuteronomy 10:18); He

"executes justice for the oppressed" and also "for the poor" (Psalm 146:7; 140:12). Indeed, God Himself said, "For I, the Lord, love justice" (Isaiah 61:8). "All His ways are justice" (Deuteronomy 32:4); and neither "will the Almighty pervert justice" (Job 34:12). "For we must all appear before the judgment seat of Christ, that each one may receive the things done in the body, according to what he has done, whether good or bad" (2 Corinthians 5:10); "God will bring every work into judgment, including every secret thing, whether good or evil" (Ecclesiastes 12:14).

This is absolute truth. But note that it is God who executes justice—not us. Said the Lord, "Vengeance is Mine, and recompense" (Deuteronomy 32:35). God is the One who will put all things right. Scripture discloses that God has set a date for that to occur—not now, but ultimately at the end of the world: "Their foot *shall* slip in due time; for the day of their calamity is at hand, and the things to come hasten upon them" (emphasis mine); "He *shall* judge the world in righteousness, and He *shall* administer judgment for the peoples in uprightness" (Psalm 9:8, emphasis mine). "Shall God not avenge His own elect who cry out day and night to Him …? I tell you that He *will* avenge them speedily" (Luke 18:7, 8, emphasis mine).

There is a reason for this: Do sin-sick humans know what is just and what is not? Do we know why some people act mean and nasty? Can we see into their hearts? No, but God can—and does.

If you're sitting in your car at a stoplight, minding your own business, and the car behind you suddenly bangs into your rear bumper, naturally you would think the fault to be the other driver's. But then, as you angrily get out of your car and walk toward the other car, you suddenly see a third car, which actually plowed into the car behind you, causing that car to bump into your car. That's a three-car pile-up, but from your first perspective, all you saw was the car that hit you.

What does it mean when you take the law into your own hands? You are saying that your way is better than God's, that you know more than He does about the situation. You are putting your faith in your own merits and in your own works. Just like the person with the legalistic mindset, you are making yourself the judge above the Judge of the universe.

Crime and Punishment

You might be wondering, then, if forgiveness means sweeping wrongs under the rug. It does not. If your teenage daughter is stealing money from you every week to buy drugs, do you keep

leaving cash lying around the house? No! Doing so would feed her habit; it would be aiding and abetting her sin.

Nowadays, confrontation is a bad word. But confrontation is biblical—as long as it is done in a right spirit. Jesus said, "If your brother sins against you, rebuke him; and if he repents, forgive him" (17:3). Be ready to forgive; want to forgive. "If your brother sins against you, go and tell him his fault between you and him alone" (Matthew 18:15). In fact, give your brother several opportunities to repent (vv. 16, 17). Be generous; be gracious toward him. Don't hold grudges. Do all in your power to prevent him from drifting from God. And realize that in some cases, that might mean allowing that person to experience consequences.

Similarly, forgiveness does not always mean that life remains at the status quo. In an abusive relationship, the one being abused does not stay in that relationship. But ending contact with an abuser also does not mean that you cannot forgive him; forgiving your abuser does not mean that you continue to receive the abuse. Forgiveness does not have to equal trust.

I have spoken with people who were sexually abused by family members when they were children. This is a horrible violation. Is forgiveness still possible? Yes, by the grace of God. By no means is this easy. Each of us knows that you don't simply

snap your fingers and suddenly all those deeply painful feelings go away. Do not give up; "pray without ceasing" (1 Thessalonians 5:17). It takes time—and always supernatural help.

Ultimately, realize that holding onto the pain and bitter hatred will hurt only one person—the one who is reliving that past injury. We become what we behold, for our own good or to our own detriment. Unforgiveness is an acid that destroys its container. It is only by turning away from ourselves and looking to Jesus that we can be made whole: "A merry heart does good, like medicine, but a broken spirit dries the bones" (Proverbs 17:22). By forgiving, you are not opening yourself up to being a victim again. In fact, you are gaining victory through Christ Jesus.

Bitter Fruit

There once was a man named McGillicuddy who was feuding with his neighbor. Whenever an opportunity arose to badger his neighbor, McGillicuddy would take advantage of it.

One night, McGillicuddy had a dream: An angel visited him and granted him a unique opportunity: "Whatever you ask me, I shall give it to you. However, I will also give to your neighbor twice what you ask."

McGillicuddy wrestled with this. He could not bear the thought of the neighbor whom he hated so much receiving a double portion of whatever he received. Finally, as a sinister smile curled across his face, he made his decision: "I pray that the angel takes one of my eyes!"

Has your vengeance burrowed so deep that you would injure yourself just to injure that other person? "When you seek revenge, you actually dig two graves," one well-known Chinese proverb explains. If you succeed, one grave will house your enemy; the other will house you. Scripture says, "Whoever digs a pit will fall into it, and he who rolls a stone will have it roll back on him" (Proverbs 26:27).

A 10-year-old boy was sitting on a park bench. A pained and angry countenance painted his face. A passerby asked him what was wrong. The young boy replied, "I'm sitting on a hornet."

The man asked urgently, "Then why don't you get up?"

The boy replied, "Because I figure I'm hurting him more than he is hurting me!"

How many of us handle forgiveness like this boy? We endure pain for the sadistic satisfaction of believing we are hurting our offender more than he is hurting us. When we get off the bench of unforgiveness, both parties can begin to experience relief.

Haman was a man consumed with revenge. His nemesis, a Jew named Mordecai, never "paid homage to Haman" (Esther 3:2), an important royal official, and it rankled Haman's ego to the point where he "was filled with wrath" (v. 5). So bent was he on his rage that he conjured a whole plot to exterminate Mordecai's entire race (v. 6), and, as though that were not enough, he even took pains to have a personal 75-foot-high gallows built for Mordecai (5:14). But in the end, for all his intentions, Haman's plan backfired on him—he was the one who was "hanged … on the gallows that he had prepared for Mordecai" (7:10).

The moral of the story? In our bid to get what we believe to be satisfactory vengeance, we might actually be losing eternal life.

Forget About It

This may come as a surprise, but forgiving someone who has wronged you is entirely up to you. In fact, you don't even need that other person to ask for forgiveness before you forgive him or her. It is your choice.

Clara Barton, who founded the American Red Cross, was in conversation with a friend one day. The friend decided to bring up a previous incident in which Clara was treated rather poorly by someone else. Clara remained silent on the subject.

"Don't you remember?" the gossiping friend continued to prod.

"No," replied Clara, "I distinctly remember forgetting it."

It is your choice to forget another's offense to you. Now, let's be clear: This doesn't mean that you suddenly have selective amnesia. There is no partial lobotomy happening here. Memories of the painful offense may come, but you choose to not dwell on them. Martin Luther said, "You cannot keep birds from flying over your head, but you can keep them from building a nest in your hair." What other people do to you is out of your control; how you react to what they do is not.

You forget the offense in this sense: You don't chew on it; you don't agonize over it day in, day out. You let it go—just as the Lord has decided to do for you: "I will not remember your sins" (Isaiah 43:25); "their sin I will remember no more" (Jeremiah 31:34).

Time Will Tell

God sees not only all angles but throughout all time too, "declaring the end from the beginning, and from ancient times things that are not yet done" (Isaiah 46:10). Our view, by contrast, is a thin slice of light in a door cracked ajar. What did the prophet Isaiah think in the moments before

he was put to death by Manasseh, Judah's idolatrous king? Did he know that one day Manasseh would be dramatically converted and return to the Lord after being taken into captivity in Babylon? (2 Chronicles 33:11–16).

Did Stephen know that Saul would become the apostle to the Gentiles? All he knew at the time was that "Saul was consenting to his death" (Acts 8:1). Stephen's martyrdom, next to Christ's, was one of the most glaring acts of injustice recounted in the Bible. But Stephen's reaction to his enemies is crucial. He did not pray for God to rain down fire on those stoning him; neither did he ask to be avenged of them. He merely "knelt down and cried out with a loud voice, 'Lord, do not charge them with this sin'" (7:60). He prayed for his persecutors; he prayed for their eternal lives.

Where did Stephen get that power? As Christ was being crucified, He uttered not one word in His own defense. Though "He was oppressed and He was afflicted, yet He opened not His mouth; … as a sheep before its shearers is silent, so He opened not His mouth" (Isaiah 53:7); "when He was reviled, [He] did not revile in return; when He suffered, He did not threaten, but committed Himself to Him who judges righteously" (1 Peter 2:23). When Christ did speak, it was out of love for those who put Him to death: "Father,

forgive them, for they do not know what they do" (Luke 23:34). Christ on the cross, dying the most agonizing of deaths, interceded for His murderers. For Jesus, "loving your enemies" was not a metaphor. A nearby Roman centurion who had been watching Jesus' patience, love, and forgiveness was ultimately converted by what he saw (Mark 15:39). Stephen's power to forgive came from Christ abiding within him.

Why didn't Jesus protest? Why didn't He do anything? Of anyone, Jesus Christ—God with us—had the right to climb down from that cross and take vengeance on those who humiliated Him. But if He had, that would have meant eternal death for each of us—which, in actuality, would have been the just thing to do. Remember, we are supposed to die for our sins (Romans 6:23).

But the fulfillment of this greatest of injustices means that we each can be "justified by faith" in Jesus (5:1). Christ's singular objective was to make a path so that every human being could be given eternal life: "The Lord ... is longsuffering toward us, not willing that any should perish but that all should come to repentance" (2 Peter 3:9). This is the reason for what may look in our eyes to be silence, to be inaction or unfairness on God's part. It may look to you as though God is doing nothing, but God is actually doing everything He can to save as many as possible. Perhaps it's someone

you know; perhaps it's your enemy; perhaps it's even yourself.

When you are getting what is owed to you, when you are fighting for your rights, when you are making sure things are fair and equal, when you retaliate verbally, who are you thinking about? Are you thinking about the one who is taking away your rights? Are you doing your utmost for his soul?

Our True Enemy

Remember who our true enemy is.

In 1805, during the Battle of Trafalgar, the famous British Admiral Horatio Nelson overheard two commanders in disagreement with each other. He promptly called them both on deck and pointed to the French ships opposite them. He told them, "Gentlemen, there is the enemy. Now shake hands and be friends." Admiral Nelson, though he lost his life, won that battle for Britain.

Scripture clearly defines our enemy: "Your adversary [is] the devil" (1 Peter 5:8). In the Parable of the Wheat and the Tares, Jesus explained that "the enemy who sowed [the tares] is the devil" (Matthew 13:39). When Jesus disclosed to His disciples His future death and resurrection, "Peter took Him aside and began to rebuke Him" (Mark 8:32). But Christ, in turn, "rebuked Peter,

saying, 'Get behind Me, Satan!'" (v. 33). The Savior had used these exact words to combat the devil in the wilderness (Luke 4:8). Peter, blinded by his own longing for glory, had acted the part of the tempter. Christ, though, knew from whom the attack had originated, and while He chastised His disciple, He simultaneously exposed the true enemy, Satan.

Thus, remember who it is that we are really fighting and against whom we are to unite. We are patriots of one country, the heavenly kingdom; "[we] are no longer strangers and foreigners, but fellow citizens with the saints" (Ephesians 2:19). We as a unit are to put on the armor of God, for "[we] are the body of Christ, and members individually" (1 Corinthians 12:27).

Every time you decide to forgive someone, you are actually dealing another blow to the adversary of souls; you are "[overcoming] evil with good" (Romans 12:21). Solomon counseled, "If your enemy is hungry, give him bread to eat; and if he is thirsty, give him water to drink" (Proverbs 25:21). Why? In so doing, "you will heap coals of fire on his head" (v. 22). You will effectively be making it as difficult as possible for him to want to treat you as his enemy. His conscience will smite him; every fiber of his being will desire to be endeared to you instead.

When Stephen prayed for the souls of his murderers, do you think that touched the heart of Paul while he stood by? (Acts 22:20). When Christ asked God the Father to forgive His executioners, what must it have done to the heart of the centurion standing watch at the cross?

And isn't that the ultimate purpose? We want their souls to be saved! We want them to be reconciled to God. The person who is the target of your bitterness is also a soul who needs saving. And God might just be using you to help convert him. This is the miracle of forgiveness: seeing your enemy as a soul lost in the bonds of Satan.

In the days of the prophet Elisha, the nations of Syria and Israel were at war. During one remarkable encounter, the Lord blinded the Syrian army and had the prophet lead the army straight into its enemy's hands (2 Kings 6:8–20).

"Shall I kill them? Shall I kill them?" asked the king of Israel excitedly (v. 21). You can almost imagine him rubbing his palms with glee.

But see Elisha's response: "You shall not kill them. Would you kill those whom you have taken captive with your sword and your bow? Set food and water before them, that they may eat and drink and go to their master" (v. 22).

And because the king of Israel listened to the prophet's merciful instruction, the Scriptures record, "The bands of Syrian raiders came no more

into the land of Israel" (v. 23). This act of mercy on the part of Israel preserved the nation; more than that, it demonstrated to a people estranged from God what their Creator was really like.

Years ago, a group of Christian missionaries in China lived in a village embedded into a steep hillside; lower down on that hill was another larger village filled with pagans. Those who lived on that hill farmed rice planted in terraces. Every day, the villagers and missionaries would hike down to the river at the bottom of the hill and fill buckets with water for their rice paddies. The missionaries, since they lived higher up on the hill, had a longer, exhausting journey. They would carry those heavy buckets on their backs past the pagan village, all the way up to a dam that irrigated their crops. It was hard work, to say the least.

Now, the pagans in the village below hated the missionaries, calling them "white devils." Late one night, some of the pagans snuck into the missionaries' village and made a cut in their dam so that the water would drain straight into their own reservoir. That got them free water and free labor, all at the expense of their enemies.

Upon discovering this and consulting together, the missionaries did not put up a fuss. They did not confront their hateful neighbors, nor did they retaliate. Months passed, and during that time, as their dam was frequently drained, they

simply had to haul more and more water up the hot trail to keep their rice and vegetables alive. But they couldn't go on doing that forever. So they prayed, asking the Lord for guidance. And the Lord answered their prayer in an unexpected way.

The next day, the leaders of the mission had the strongest impression to intentionally water not just their own paddies but those of their pagan neighbors first. So, they hiked all the way down to the river and carried those full, heavy buckets of water back up the hill and into their neighbors' fields. Then, at the end of the day, beyond exhausted, they trudged back down to the river, filled their buckets again, and hauled them all the way back up the hill, past the pagan village, to their own rice paddies. As the pagans watched in disbelief, their hearts were overcome with shame. They were mystified; they could not understand.

"Why are you being so good to us?" they demanded to know. "Tell us about your God!"

Hearts are not moved by acts of revenge; that is what any sinner would do. Hearts are moved—they are transformed—by acts of forgiveness. Give your enemies every opportunity to see the forgiveness of Christ: "Love your enemies, bless those who curse you, do good to those who hate you, and pray for those who spitefully use you and persecute you" (Matthew 5:44). "Repay no one evil for evil" (Romans 12:17); "do not avenge

yourselves" (v. 19). Paul said, "If it is possible, as much as depends on you, live peaceably with all men" (v. 18). Do it, he said, "giving preference to one another" (v. 10). Be of "a good conscience, that when they defame you as evildoers, those who revile your good conduct in Christ may be ashamed" (1 Peter 3:16). Give no excuse to defame your character, lest you injure the cause of God.

David, while being hunted by King Saul, had more than one chance to slay his persecutor. Some even think he had every right to. But on both occasions, David refrained (1 Samuel 24:10; 26:11). And each time, David's mercy caused Saul to rebuke himself (24:16, 17; 26:21). But even with all of these extra opportunities given him, Saul ultimately ceased to repent. That was his choice. As for David, he had made certain that he was blameless in that. David did all that he could to turn Saul's heart. By his own willingness to forgive, he washed his hands clean of the king's blood.

How much more, then, does God do to turn each and every one of us to repentance? How much more forbearance does He have? How much more love for our souls?

Chapter 7

The Devil in Church

Let's get a little personal here. Are there people who stop attending church because someone has offended them? I know there are.

What is most difficult to accept is that the offense happened in church; it happened with someone who is supposed to be a Christian and supposed to behave as Christ did. There tends to be an assumption that all unkind behavior occurs only outside of the church.

Yes, we are supposed to be the light of the world; we are supposed to represent Christ. But the fact of the matter is that the church is full of recovering sinners. This should come as no surprise; Jesus told us as much: "Those who are well have no need of a physician, but those who are sick. I have not come to call the righteous, but sinners, to repentance" (Luke 5:31, 32). This sickness was in the early church: Paul said, "After my

departure savage wolves will come in among you, not sparing the flock" (Acts 20:29). This sickness is in our church today, and just as in apostolic times, it can be healed only by the Great Physician.

Spiritual Dementia

You've probably heard it said many a time: Hurt people hurt people. Sometimes, they may not even mean to hurt you. You just happen to be collateral damage. Does it make their wrong okay? No. As Christians, we should not be too embarrassed or too proud to own up to the wrongs we have caused. But even if your brother or sister does not admit his or her fault, does it mean you can't forgive him or her?

Now use your imagination for a moment. Suppose you're invited to lunch at a church member's home for the first time. After church, you make your way over and ring the doorbell. After the church member answers, she takes your coat and asks you to have a seat in the living room while she finishes preparing the meal. Then, she heads down the hallway and into the kitchen, leaving you alone on the sofa.

The next thing you know, an elderly gentleman walks into the room. He comes right up to you and gets in your face and says, "All these ugly people always coming into my house! In fact, I've never

seen someone as ugly as you. And you just came here to eat our food. You pigs just come here to eat all our food!"

Naturally, you're upset. You jump up and march down the hallway and into the kitchen, demanding the hostess retrieve your coat so that you can storm out of the house.

Astonished, the church member asks, "Why?"

You then proceed to tell her about the rude, old man who insulted you right to your face.

She answers, "Oh, I am so sorry about that! That's grandpa. I didn't realize he had woken up from his nap. Grandpa has severe dementia, you see. The sad thing is that he used to be the nicest guy in the world before he got sick—but now …"

And, of course, everything changes now that you realize that the person who insulted you has dementia, a sickness. You return to the living room and happily stay for lunch—though you're careful not to take a seat next to grandpa.

In that scenario, how you decided to react to the insult changed once you were provided with one piece of information: The offender was unwell. He did not even realize what he was saying. In much the same way, a person who has been damaged mentally or emotionally or, most of all, spiritually isn't thinking of other people. He's probably just struggling with the demons within.

Here's another example: There once was a pastor who had some time to kill at the airport before his departure. As he was strolling around the terminal, he saw a young boy at a shoeshine station. Wanting to support the industrious lad, he decided to pay for a shoeshine. But he was soon very sorry for it.

Once he sat down, the boy immediately got to work, but it was the sloppiest, most incompetent job ever. The boy smudged polish on the pastor's socks and on his shoelaces. He attempted a spit shine, but the spit landed everywhere except on the pastor's shoes. The pastor was growing livid. He stopped the boy and said angrily, "Look at the mess you've made! You've got polish on my socks and spit on my pants. I can't believe the airport allows you in here. You actually want me to pay for this?"

For the first time the boy looked up at the pastor, and the pastor suddenly noticed that his eyes were red and swollen. "I'm so sorry, sir," the child replied. "My mother died last week, and I cried a lot and got an eye infection in both eyes. I can't see very well right now, but I have to work. I have to feed my little brother and sister."

That changed everything for the pastor. He had seen only the mess on the outside, not any of the hurt on the inside. Once his eyes were opened, the pastor's anger instantly turned to pity. He was

no longer thinking of what the boy had done to him; he was thinking of what the boy was going through. He paid for the shoeshine with a generous tip.

How often are we like that pastor, pointing out the bad behavior without understanding the reasons behind the behavior? How often do we treat the symptoms instead of dealing with the root cause?

Friendly Fire

In 1991, at the end of the first Gulf War, 149 Americans had been killed. Sadly, 31 percent died from so-called friendly fire. Scripture has already warned us, "The devil has come down to you, having great wrath, because he knows that he has a short time" (Revelation 12:12). Satan is on the warpath, and one of the most effective strategies he uses is infiltration: divide and conquer. What better location to attack than in our home base, the church?

If a stranger passing me on the street stopped, pointed at me, and mocked my bald head, I wouldn't care that much. But if one of my good friends did it, that would sting a bit. The verse above states that it was time for Satan to start pulling out all the stops, so it only makes sense that he

is going to go for where it really hurts. And where it really hurts is where you are most vulnerable.

It was Joseph's own brothers who sold him as a slave. Absalom, David's eldest, murdered his half-brother and later attempted to take not only his father's throne but his life as well. Luke 22:3, 6 state, "Then Satan entered Judas, surnamed Iscariot, who was numbered among the twelve. … So he … sought opportunity to betray [Jesus]."

Note that this does not mean that Judas had no control over his decisions; he had long since been harboring the same kind of dissatisfaction with the Savior's methods as Satan had with God's government in heaven. As Paul taught, "Whom you present yourselves slaves to obey, you are that one's slaves whom you obey" (Romans 6:16). Judas, in essence, had given himself over to the power of the devil.

When Judas betrayed Jesus, the Lord asked His wayward disciple, "Friend, why have you come?" (Matthew 26:50). Of Christ it is prophesied: "'What are these wounds between your arms?' Then he will answer, 'Those with which I was wounded in the house of my friends'" (Zechariah 13:6). "Even my own familiar friend in whom I trusted, who ate my bread, has lifted up his heel against me" (Psalm 41:9).

The Savior was betrayed by one of the 12 men—the head elder, you could say—who

walked most closely with Him on this earth. If Satan hit Christ where it deeply hurt, what makes us think he is not doing the same to us? Jesus taught, "A servant is not greater than his master" (John 15:20). If you had been alive at that time, would you have been a member of the "church" Jesus shepherded, or would you have ducked out to avoid the friendly fire?

I'm Outta Here

You might be surprised to find out that the Bible recounts an incident in which a well-known prophet called it quits on his "church." The prophet Elijah spent years in the midst of his backslidden generation, battling against idolatry in Israel. Through him, God wrought many wonders and, by a miracle of fire called down on Mount Carmel, repentance in His chosen people (1 Kings 18:20–39). Finally, Elijah could claim the victory. God then further blessed, sending an "abundance of rain" (v. 41) and thereby ending a multi-year drought.

However, there was someone who was not so happy with this turn of events: Israel's own queen. In response to an angry death threat sent by Queen Jezebel, Elijah took off running—literally (19:2, 3). He left everything and fled far into the wilderness, scared, panicked, and deeply discouraged (v. 4).

But God visited his wayward prophet. "What are you doing here, Elijah?" the Lord asked (v. 9). In other words, why had Elijah abandoned the church?

Then came the excuses: "I have been very zealous for the LORD God of hosts," Elijah started off (v. 10). ("Just because I've stopped going to church doesn't mean I've abandoned God," a person in today's world might say.) "The children of Israel have forsaken Your covenant, torn down Your altars, and killed Your prophets with the sword," was his next reason. ("My church is in full apostasy. You should've seen the way they held the service. And don't even get me started on the pastor's sermons. How could I stay in a church like that?" that same person might say.) "I alone am left; and they seek to take my life," concluded Elijah. ("I was the only one in that whole congregation on fire. I was the only one standing up for the truth. And everyone saw me as a troublemaker, and none of them liked me, and they didn't want me there. So, I left!")

Have people told you similar reasons as to why they stopped going to church?

The Lord's reply to Elijah's complaints was simple: "Go, return" (v. 15). That is God's answer to any who have been offended by the church. Christ commissioned us, "Go into all the world and preach the gospel to every creature" (Mark 16:15).

We have a God-given duty to reach others for the kingdom of heaven—and that includes those inside our own church. Elijah was the Lord's messenger, sent to bring revival to God's people. But it's hard to bail water from a boat when you're in the ocean instead; it's hard to clean house when you're on the street in front of it.

God made known to His prophet that his perspective had skewed his feelings: "Yet I have reserved seven thousand in Israel, all whose knees have not bowed to Baal, and every mouth that has not kissed him" (1 Kings 19:18). Elijah had mistakenly assumed that he was the only one faithful to God, and in so doing, he had resigned to consign Israel to a fate of torment. How quickly he had forgotten God's miracles! How easily we can dismiss God's work when wallowing in self-pity.

Theodore Roosevelt was a budding politician when tragedy struck. On February 14, 1884, both his mother and his young wife, while giving birth, died. Roosevelt had especially cherished his wife, Alice, writing this in regard to her premature death: "The light has gone out of my life." From that point on, he never spoke about her, but in his broken grief, he forsook politics and fled to the Badlands of North Dakota to become a cowboy. But two years later, in 1886, Roosevelt was coaxed back into running for governor of New York City

and eventually became one of the greatest U.S. presidents our country has ever known.

God had a plan for his life—and God has one for each of us. If Roosevelt had remained in the Dakota Badlands, America might not have become what it did. If we remain out of the church, we might actually be fighting against the very purpose to which God has called us.

No Pain, No Gain

It is a fact that loving someone means taking a risk. If you choose to trust a person and open up to him, there is always a chance that he might betray your confidence or slight your love or hurt you in some way. People often fail one another. But that doesn't mean we stop loving people. We endure through the growing pains because the outcome can be worth so much more than the hurt.

The backcountry of Nevada is known as a top spot for rockhounding, or, basically, hunting for rocks. When I go camping there, it's easy to see all sorts of precious stones dotted about the terrain. They are bright and colorful, but they are also quite rough, with lots of sharp edges. Often, rockhounds collect these stones and take them to a nearby rock shop to be put in a rock tumbler. There, the stones are poured into the tumbler along with a grinding solution. Then, the machine

is turned on—and begins making the most awful ruckus!

But it has to—because that is the only way all of those jagged, misshapen rocks are ever going to get polished. They're scraping and knocking against one another over and over again, and when the machine is finally finished, out come all of these beautifully round, shiny gems. But in order to look that way, they each had to go through that not-so-nice process.

The church is akin to that rock tumbler. If a rock falls out of that tumbler, it's going to stay rough around the edges. It needs to stay in the tumbler in order to be refined—jostling against the other rocks. In his first epistle, Peter likened Christians to "living stones, … being built up a spiritual house" (2:5). We need to stay in the church in order for God to sanctify us. How else can all those "living stones" fit together to construct that "spiritual house"?

Did you notice that all—not just some—of the rocks in the tumbler are rough? There may be times when you're not the only one who is hurt; maybe the brother or sister who hurt you was also hurt *by* you. Instead of sitting there waiting for the other person to come to you, what if you were to take the initiative to apologize first? The point is not who is right; the point is to humble ourselves and love one other.

If I were to choose between being a horse or a donkey, I'd choose a horse. Do you know why? When a herd of thoroughbred horses is surrounded by a pack of wolves, the horses form a circle with their heads all in the center. As the wolves approach them, the horses kick out their hind legs, working together to form a defensive barrier against the predators.

However, I understand that when a herd of donkeys is attacked, they do the opposite. They form a circle with their heads on the outside and their backsides together. When a predator approaches them, the donkeys get nervous and start kicking one another.

That's often how the church behaves, isn't it? We try to take on the devil on our own, but we just end up hurting one another. What would happen if we put our heads together instead? What if our arms were reached out in forgiveness? What if we were watching out for one another in compassion? What if we gathered more often in prayer than gossip? "Bear one another's burdens" (Galatians 6:2); "comfort each other and edify one another" (1 Thessalonians 5:11); "be at peace among yourselves" (v. 13); "blessed are the peacemakers, for they shall be called sons of God" (Matthew 5:9). Peter instructed, "All of you be submissive to one another, and be clothed with

humility" (1 Peter 5:5). "Submit to God" first; then, you will be able to "resist the devil" (James 4:7).

I'd like to set a challenge for you right now: The next time you attend church, step foot inside with this prayer foremost in your mind: "Lord, show me who You would like me to minister to today. Teach me how to show them Your love."

Chapter 8

The Keys to the Kingdom

Scripture summarizes the truth of forgiveness for us: "What does the LORD require of you but to do justly, to love mercy, and to walk humbly with your God?" (Micah 6:8). "Do justly": Don't put yourself in the position to have to ask for forgiveness. "Love mercy": But if someone has wronged you, forgive them readily. "Walk humbly with your God": Remember the Lord has forgiven you "10,000 talents," which makes it easier for you to forgive others.

So, why is forgiveness so crucial for a Christian?

Two great pillars of the Renaissance, Leonardo da Vinci and Michelangelo Buonarroti, were life-long rivals, and their feud was made all the more incendiary because of the artists' celebrity. At one point, they were even trading insults in the form of open letters.

During this time, Leonardo had been commissioned to paint *The Last Supper*, now one of the most famous murals in history. In the painting, Jesus sits in the center; on either side of Him are the 12 apostles, with Judas on the left of the Savior.

As Leonardo started the face of Judas, he had the sinister idea to paint in Michelangelo's face instead of using an anonymous model, as he usually did. He relished the onlookers who passed by and gasped at what he was doing. This revenge took the cake, immortalizing Michelangelo as a greedy, cowardly traitor.

But now he came to the last face to be painted, the face of Jesus, and something strange happened. He just could not get that face right, no matter how hard he tried. He would paint and blot it out, paint and blot out. He went through several models. Everything else was complete—except the Savior's face. Finally, in desperation, he prayed, "Lord, help me to see Your face!"

Then the answer came to his heart: "You will never see the face of Jesus until you change the face of Judas."

We will never see the face of Jesus if we cannot exercise the gift of forgiveness: "Pursue peace with all people, and holiness, without which no one will see the Lord" (Hebrews 12:14). For the believer forgiveness isn't an option; it is mandatory. So,

Leonardo blotted out his rival from off the face of Judas and painted in the one we know today.

Lacking the Spirit

In the days before Christ's second coming, He has promised to give us "the latter rain" (Joel 2:23), the outpouring of His Holy Spirit (v. 29). A revival more powerful than we can imagine will sweep the planet.

The latter rain is yet to come, but we must make ready now in order to be able to receive it. It will come in like manner as the former rain, known as the Day of Pentecost. This was the day in which the Holy Spirit was given to the small band of 120 early believers, culminating in the establishment of the Christian church (Acts 2:1–4).

To receive this former rain, Christ's disciples prepared in a very specific manner: They spent their hours together in "one accord in prayer and supplication" (1:14). Scripture tells us that when the Holy Spirit actually came upon them, they were still in this same posture, "with one accord in one place" (2:1).

Did you catch that? They were in accordance with one another. There were no disagreements among them; they were entirely reconciled to one another. This is significant because prior to Jesus' crucifixion, the apostles were bickering among

themselves as to which of them was the greatest (Luke 22:24). But now all of their trespasses, their offenses, their injustices—all had been forgiven.

Forgiveness was the requirement to receive the Holy Spirit. The Spirit does not exist "where there are envy, strife, and divisions" (1 Corinthians 3:3); He will not stay in such an atmosphere.

Note also the specific manner in which they came to be in accord with one another. They prayed together: "Confess your trespasses to one another, and pray for one another, that you may be healed" (James 5:16). In the process of forgiveness, an investment of prayer is indispensable. You confess to God through prayer; you intercede for one another through prayer. What was Daniel doing just before receiving the prophetic vision of the 490-year prophecy? He was in prayer (Daniel 9:3).

The same is required of us today in order to receive the latter rain. We need to be cultivating that same character of humility, of vulnerability, of surrender. We need to be asking forgiveness of God, and we need to be forgiving one another: "By this all will know that [we] are [Christ's] disciples, if [we] have love for one another" (John 13:35).

Settling Accounts

"The time is near," declares Revelation 1:3.

The latter rain will stand in stark contrast to the devil's counterfeit revival in a final battle that will usher in the very end of the world. In these last days of Earth's history, the devil is waging all-out war against the people of God. During this time, we will likely witness some of the most heinous injustices the world has seen, "a time of trouble, such as never was" (Daniel 12:1). God's people will be falsely accused of breaking His law—when they are, in actuality, the only ones keeping it. The remnant will be seen as traitors, as enemies of the state; their reputations will be shot, their life's work dragged through the mud. (See Revelation 13:11–18.)

Will you stand among this group? What will be your reaction to what is done to you? Will it be one of vengeance and retaliation? Will you fight to the death for what is rightfully owed you? Or will you be a witness for Christ in the culmination of this great controversy between the Lord and Satan?

In these final days, your character will likely be put to the test more than ever. This is the time above all others that God will display a people on earth totally surrendered to Him. Do you believe it? It is prophesied in Scripture: These people will

have the mind of Christ, God's name—His character—"written on their foreheads" (14:1). They will "follow the Lamb wherever He goes" (v. 4); they will be Spirit-filled and "without fault before the throne of God" (v. 5). God's character will be perfectly recreated in them. How is this possible?

The injunction has already been given us. In the days before Christ's first coming, in preparation for His public ministry, John the Baptist, His forerunner, preached a very specific message: "Repent, for the kingdom of heaven is at hand!" (Matthew 3:2). Ask, receive, and offer forgiveness. This same message is the one repeated for Christ's second coming: Repent.

We are currently living in these latter days, the short time before Christ's advent. Scripture plainly shows this time is now a parallel of the Jewish nation's Day of Atonement, a ceremony that God gave to represent the final day of judgment. In this ceremony, observed once a year, the people were symbolically cleansed from their sins. All those who in earnestness confessed and repented of their sins—a practice known as "[afflicting] your souls" (Leviticus 16:29)—would have their sins cleansed by the blood of the Lord's goat offered in the temple, a symbol for Christ's sacrifice. Those who did not repent were held responsible for their sins and were "cut off from [their] people" (23:29).

It was a most solemn, most important ritual that served to point toward that final day when Christ will settle all accounts in the heavenly courts. As it was in the typical Day of Atonement, so it shall be on the real judgment day: All those who have afflicted their souls, examining themselves (2 Corinthians 13:5), in humility bringing their sins to God to be forgiven and covered by the blood of Jesus, will have their iniquities expunged from their records for good. But those who have not repented will be charged with the sins they have done and will be sentenced accordingly. These people will be eternally "cut off" from God.

The judgment is all or nothing: You are saved, or you are lost. Either you are fully forgiven, or you are fully not. There is no halfway point. This is the key to God's kingdom: forgiveness—receiving God's forgiveness and passing it on. Jesus' words could not be clearer:

> If you forgive men their trespasses, your heavenly Father will also forgive you. But if you do not forgive men their trespasses, neither will your Father forgive your trespasses" (Matthew 6:14, 15).

This is the living gospel: *forgiveness*. If we don't understand this, if we have no practical nor personal experience of it, if it is not actuated in the

life, then we are missing the whole point. Christ's life, death, and resurrection is the most beautiful act of forgiveness the world will ever know. It is through living the reality of His forgiveness that we will "become blameless and harmless, children of God without fault in the midst of a crooked and perverse generation, among whom [we] shine as lights in the world" (Philippians 2:15).

The day of judgment will come. On that day, the books will be opened, the debts stricken, all accounts settled—for eternity. But your record on that day is determined by a decision made *today*. And it is made by answering one simple question: Do you want to be forgiven?

The Burden Lifted

In conclusion, I'd like to return to our Parable of the Unforgiving Servant. This man, whom we called Sidney, owed the king 10,000 talents—in today's currency, several billion dollars. He had squandered his master's money. As the debt mounted, surely in the back of his mind, he must have known someday there would be an accounting, a judgment, a reckoning, and maybe even severe punishment. How could he ever have peace?

If you were offered $10 million to spend on all the pleasures of the world in Vegas for 90 days,

you might be tempted until you saw the fine print: At the end of 90 days, you will be thrown in the fire and burned for 20 minutes. How could you ever enjoy a single day of pleasure knowing you are one day closer to the firepit?

Sidney must have been tormented in his mind, weighed down living with the guilt and knowledge that a day of judgment and punishment was coming. Are you in that same throng of torment? Are you desperate for peace? We are now suffering under the weight of our sins, and the devil is doing all he can to make sure we ignore the fine print.

But we need to look to live. The miracle of a recreated, transformed, converted heart is available to us now. It happens only when we kneel at the foot of the cross in the full realization that Jesus actually hung there, bleeding, suffering excruciating mental and physical pain, to face absolute death—in His own free will, out of love for us—for our lifetime of sins. At the cross where Jesus died is where our life can begin again. Let us not be like Sidney, who squandered not only what he did not own but also what he was freely given. Rather, in gratitude let us take up our cross and forgive as we are forgiven.

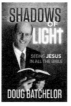